THE BRENTA DOLOMITES

A wonderful journey through the
Brenta Dolomites discovering
the Adamello Brenta Nature Reserve.

INDEX

THE DREAM MOUNTAINS

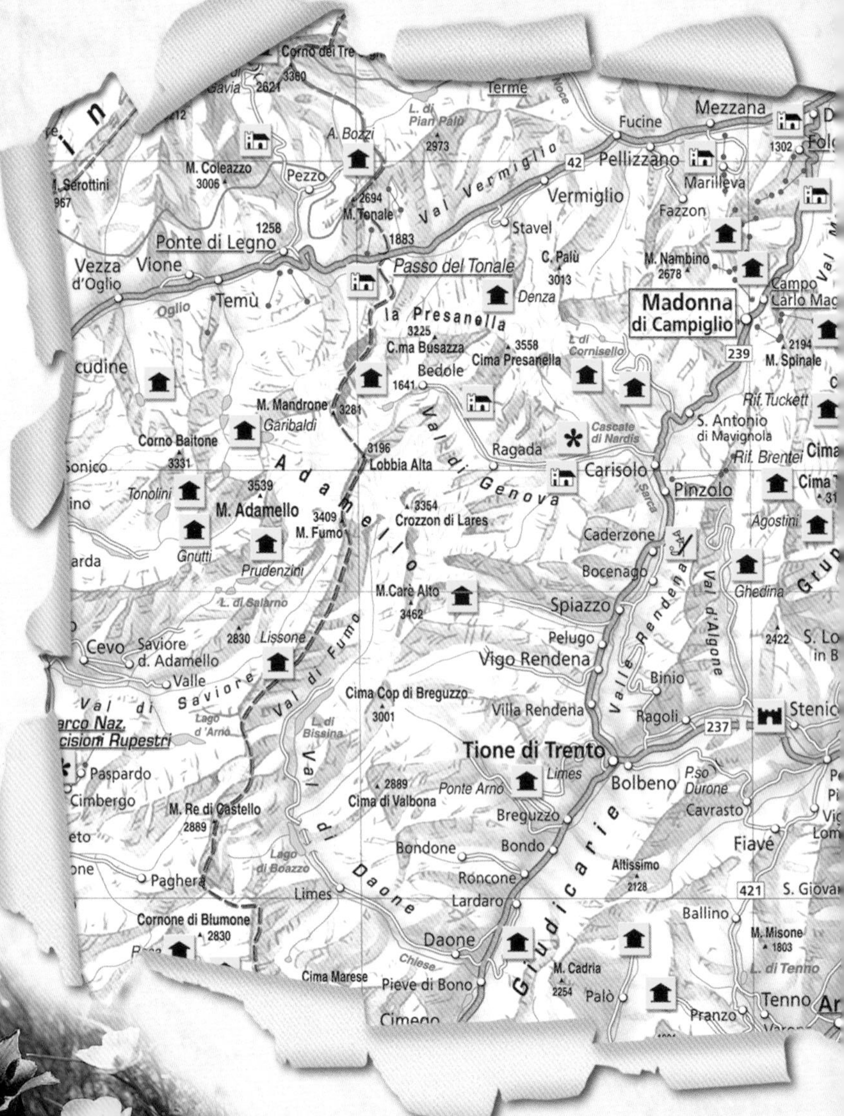

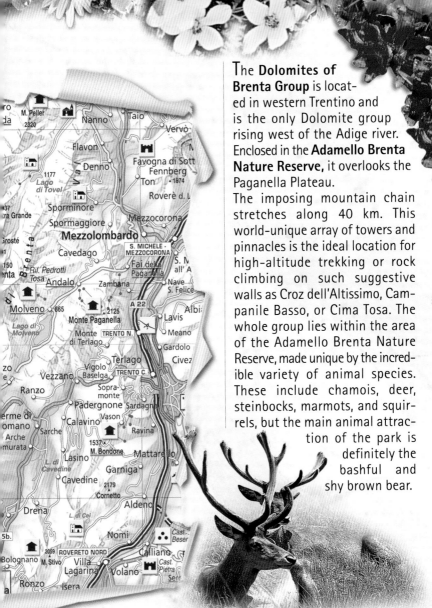

The **Dolomites of Brenta Group** is located in western Trentino and is the only Dolomite group rising west of the Adige river. Enclosed in the **Adamello Brenta Nature Reserve,** it overlooks the Paganella Plateau.

The imposing mountain chain stretches along 40 km. This world-unique array of towers and pinnacles is the ideal location for high-altitude trekking or rock climbing on such suggestive walls as Croz dell'Altissimo, Campanile Basso, or Cima Tosa. The whole group lies within the area of the Adamello Brenta Nature Reserve, made unique by the incredible variety of animal species. These include chamois, deer, steinbocks, marmots, and squirrels, but the main animal attraction of the park is definitely the bashful and shy brown bear.

The Brenta Dolomites

THE BRENTA *D*OLOMITES

The **Brenta Dolomites** are an extremely beautiful and fascinating mountain range situated in the Province of Trento.

The towns that stretch out beneath its slopes are the famous **Madonna di Campiglio, Pinzolo, Fai della Paganella, Andalo** and

The Brenta Dolomites as seen from Lake Nero

The Brenta Dolomites as seen from Presanella

Molveno. Nestled between the **Sole, Non, Rendena, Adige** and **Giudicarie Superiore valleys,** the principal rivers are the **Sarca,** to the East, and **Noce** to the North. "A forest of towers, pinnacles and peaks", was how **Cesare Battisti** (great geographer and irredentist par excellence) described the

Bocca di Brenta

Brenta Chain over a century ago; and in fact that is exactly how it looks. This impressive mountain range extends for a good 40 km and is 12 km wide. The 3173 metre high **Cima Tosa** is the highest mountain in the region, while the other principal peaks are between 2800 and 3000 metres high. This spectacular mountain setting with its glaciers, inaccessible canyons, infinite walkways,

The Tuckett Refuge

climbs and excursions, provides mountain enthusiasts with intense and enjoyable moments. There are also many famous refuges offering a warm welcome and hospitality to tired excursionists. Geographically speaking, the Brenta Dolomites form part of the **Rhaetian Alpine Range** and are separated from the

Panoramic view of Cima Brenta

The Twelve Apostles Refuge

The Grostè Pass

Tuckett Refuge, Castelletto and Cima Sella

Eastern Dolomites by a deep gully of the Adige Valley. But it is still part of the Dolomites, a name derived from **Deodat de Dolomieu,** a French geologist whose studies have helped us

Crozzon di Brenta

understand the chemical composition of one of the most unique mountain ranges in the world.

Detail of the Brentei Church

The millenary action of atmospheric agents, rivers and glaciers has left an unmistakable mark on this landscape, and is a rich testimony

The Vallesinella Waterfalls

Campanil Basso

to the complex geological evolution of planet Earth. This transformation is more than

Cima Brenta, Cima Sella and Castelletto

evident in the distinctive rock strata of the region and its unusual composition, rock formations, faults, dolina, glaciers and lakes that converge in the heart of the Brenta Range.

Rock-goats

The **Adamello Brenta Nature Reserve** was established in 1967, and covers an area of 618 square kilometres and is the largest protected area in the Trento region. It also has the largest woodland area, which covers at least one third of the protected land. The Reserve

stretches along the Brenta range in the East and the granitic massif of the **Adamello–Presanella** in the West, which are separated by the ice canyon of **Val Rendena.** As well as

the countless arboreal species such as firs, pines, larches, mountain pines, rhododendrons and azaleas, the park is also home to an abundance of unique alpine plant species, such as: alpine stars, anemones, arnica,

The Nardis Waterfalls

ranunculus, various species of lilies, and lichen.

One of the most interesting aspects of this Reserve is the fact that it is home to an incredible variety of animal life: chamois, deers, rock-goats, mouflons, marmots, squirrels, badgers and species of birds, such as: grouses, owls, partridges and the majestic

golden eagles. However, the main natural attraction of the Reserve has to be the abundance of brown bear that have made their home here. Solitary and shy, these beautiful, mysterious creatures are constantly monitored by the expert of the Adamello Brenta Reserve.

ANDALO

Andalo is situated 1040 metres above sea level, on a lush green plateau between **Paganella** and the eastern slopes of the **Brenta Dolomite** chain, surrounded by impressive coniferous forests. It is the perfect starting point for those wishing to explore the Adamello Brenta Nature Reserve. If you follow the walkway from hotel Pradel you will arrive at the **Croz dell'Altissimo Refuge,** and the **Selvata** and **then to the Pedrotti refuges.** From here—maybe after resting at one of the

M. Bondone

PAGANELLA
2125

TRENTO

1423

Santel

957

Fai della Paganella

Mezzolombardo

refuges—the more able-bodied can attempt the tiring and challenging climb to the 3173 metre Cima Tosa peak; the highest mountain in the Brenta Chain. The "normal" **Cima Tosa** route is a very demanding climb, which should only be attempted by expert

Andalo

mountaineers. Whatever your fitness or training level, when planning a mountain excursion you should always ask advice from the local alpine guides. During the winter months, Andalo is an important tourist destination and boasts a wide variety of ski slopes, including a 1200 m Olympic slope that can be reached using the modern ski lifts. The numerous hotels and refuges that are dotted all

along the slopes provide ski enthusiasts with the opportunity for endless sporting enjoyment in a unique natural habitat.

Cima Tosa

MOLVENO

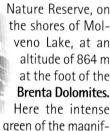

The town of Molveno is situated in the Adamello Brenta Nature Reserve, on the shores of Molveno Lake, at an altitude of 864 m at the foot of the **Brenta Dolomites.** Here the intense green of the magnificent forests reflects upon the clear blue waters of the lake creating a breathtaking ménage of colour. Molveno is an ideal starting point for those planning to explore the heart of Brenta. This busy summer holiday destination becomes a fascinating place during the winter and provides tourists with a fun and relaxing holiday experience. Molveno is also particularly beautiful during the autumn, and walkers will be enchanted by the colours of the leaves as they turn red and yellow and the silence of the woods. If you're

Molveno

Molveno Lake

really lucky, you might even have the honour of bumping into a brown bear. A truly unforgettable experience for the unsuspecting nature lover.

FAI DELLA PAGANELLA

Fai is situated on a vast precipice that overlooks the Adige valley and the slopes of **Monte Fausior.**

Thanks to its position, Fai has a particularly mild climate, even during the winter months.

Brenta as seen from the Pradel Refuge

However, as it is near to Altopiano di Andalo, winter tourism is not affected at all. In fact, Fai has many ski lifts that take skiers to the peaks of **Paganella** where they can try out the wide variety of slopes that the area has to offer.

Fai is also full of historical attractions. The remains of Raetic forts and barbed wire are still visible today.

MOLVENO – PEDROTTI REFUGE
OSVALDO ORSI WALKWAY

Here visitors will find an enthralling itinerary, not only for the natural habitat but also for the breathtaking views of some of the most renowned peaks in the Brenta mountain range. One of the most famous is **Campanil Basso,** an emblem of the Breanta range. Along this walkway you can observe the Sfulmini range and the exploits of the rope climbers. This very long highaltitude climb requires good mountaineering skills, and should only be attempted with adequate preparation, training, equipment and the correct clothing, as it is possible to come across snow even in the summer. From Molveno, along the **n. 319 footpath,** or from Andalo to the Pradel Refuge and then to the Croz dell'Altissimo Refuge, at an altitude of 1431 m, the two itineraries converge. Here you follow a

Croz dell'Altissimo

Campanil Basso

well-marked walkway that leads to the Selvata Refuge at 1630 m. At this point the walkway becomes increasingly difficult and the Pedrotti Refuge at 2490 m (where we would recommend you stay the night), can just be made out high above you in the distance. The walkway is long and tiring (roughly 4 hours from Pradel to the Pedrotti Refuge and 5 hours from Molveno), but your fatigue will be rewarded by the beautiful natural surroundings and the knowledge that you're in the best place to continue your journey the

next day. Set-off early from Pedrotti, and ascend to Bocca di Brenta, a hundred metres above the refuge. Here you will have a truly breathtaking view of Adamello to the west and the Dolomites to the east. If you follow on and turn right along the **n. 303 "Orsi" walkway,** you will pass the base of Campanil Basso, ascending onwards through peaks and pinnacles that have been named after some of the famous mountaineers who put themselves to the test on these rocks. On reaching the Tuckett mouth at an altitude of 2648 m, you then descend towards the Tuckett Refuge, where you could stop off before continuing to Brentei Refuge. From here you ascend once more to Bocca di Brenta and return to the Pedrotti Refuge.

Those who prefer a shorter and less demanding route can tackle the Orsi walkway by taking the ski lift from **Grostè** to Madonna di Campiglio.

Pedrotti Refuge

TOVEL LAKE 1177M.

An excursion in the fairytale surroundings of the Adamello Brenta Nature Reserve is a must for all those wishing to explore one of the most fascinating regions of Brenta. Situated in the Northern part of the mountain range, the area can be reached by car from **Tuenno,** in the Non valley, along the 12 km long **S.P. n.14** road that passes through a wild and untouched valley. Tovel Lake became

Tovel Lake

famous worldwide for its waters that turn red. Although this phenomenon has unfortunately not occurred since 1964, it was caused by the presence of a special kind of algae called **Glenodinium Sanguineum.** Set beneath the shadow of the Brenta peak, the lake is situated in a valley surrounded by a beautiful forest of

firs and larches. From here it is possible to reach the numerous "malga"(shepherds huts) on foot. You can visit the malga of **Termoncello, Denno, Pozzol** or **Tuena,** which are all easy and pleasurable excursions. From the lake you can also reach the heart of one of the wildest natural habitats in Brenta that stretches from **Cima Sasso Rosso** to **Cima Sassara** near Grostè. The walk to **Pracastròn Pass** is not particularly strenuous, but beyond this point it becomes increasingly difficult and should only be attempted by expert mountaineers. Between the Pass and Cima Sassara you will find the beautiful Bonvecchio picnic area at a height of 2790 m, an ideal shelter along the Costanzi walkway that leads from the Pracastròn Pass to the Graffer Refuge.

MADONNA DI CAMPIGLIO 1550 M.

Madonna di Campiglio is definitely the principal centre of the Brenta Dolomites and is one of the most visited and famous mountain destinations in the world. In fact, in the past, it was a chosen holiday destination for **Princess "Sissi"**. The main square

has been named in honour of Giovan Battista Righi who in 1872 purchased the land, where the town and the road that rises from Pinzolo now lie, and with incredible foresight he built the first hotel of the town. This small but very famous town can be found in a natural basin covered with

Presanella chains in the west. Its ideal position, altitude and fantastic snow falls make Madonna di Campiglio one of the busiest and appealing winter resorts in the entire Alpine Arc. There are numerous ski slopes at Campiglio, all of which are connected to the

woodland and is situated between the **Brenta** mountain chain in the east and the **Adamello** and

CIMA BRENTA
3150 m

CIMA SELLA
2917 m

PIETRA GRANDE
2936 m

CIMA GROSTÈ
2905

RIF.TUKETT

GROSTÈ 2500 m
RIF. GROSTÈ

RIF.
GRAFFER

MONTE SPINALE
2100 m
RIF. SPINALE

MADONNA D

STADIO
GHIAC

CAMPO CARLO MAGNO 1682 m

STADIO

PRADALAGO
2100
RIF. AGOSTI

MONTE VIGO
2180 m

MALGA VIGO
1800 m

20

Cima Sella

Folgarida and **Marilleva** region of the **Sole Valley.** In fact, there are so many, you will not have to ski on the same slope twice and could even visit them all in one day.

Vallesinella waterfalls

Madonna di Campiglio

Vallesinella Waterfall

Campiglio is also home to the **Ski World Cup** which is held on the legendary **"Tre Tre"** slope. There are also myriads of cultural events and exhibitions held here every year. In the summer months, the modern ski lifts allow visitors to explore the entire Brenta range and enjoy the numerous excursions that this incredible region has to offer. If you ascend from Pinzolo towards Campiglio, at the gate of the town near the **"fontanella",** you will find a breathtaking view of some

The Fontanella.

of the most famous peaks in the Brenta region. From Cima Tosa, Cima Brenta, Campanil Basso and Cima Sella you can make out the Tukett and Brentei refuges in the distance. To reach these well known refuges, it's a good idea to leave you car in the Vallesinella refuge's car park and take to the panoramic waterfall walkway that leads to the beautiful Casinei Refuge. Here you can take a satisfying break then continue

A snowslide on the Bocca di Tuckett

on your way turning right to reach the "Maria e Alberto ai Brentei" Refuge or left to reach the "Tuckett", "Alimonta" and "Grostè" refuges. To the north of Madonna di Campiglio, lies the **Campo Carlo Magno Pass** that connects the Rendeva Valley with the Sun Valley. In summer, the Pass is the ideal place for taking easy and enjoyable walks, or for playing golf, while in winter, it is also an ideal place for Cross-country skiing.

Boch Refuge

800 M.
℘INZOLO

Pinzolo has always been one of the main summer holiday destinations, but winter tourism is growing, thanks to the modern ski lifts and slopes that cater for all levels and requirements. Although work is currently on hold, there is a project for a route that will connect the area with the ski slopes of Campiglio. The town boasts a rich and ancient history, but due to floods and fires in the past, you will note that the architecture of the town is quite modern.

Panoramic view

Doss del Sabion

Just outside the town, you can visit the ancient San Vigilio church with its splendid bas-reliefs and frescoes. The most noteworthy is the **"Danza Macabra"** (Macabre Dance), dated 1539, and is over twenty metres long. Pinzolo was the village of the **"moleta rendeneri"** and the

Church san Vigilio

craftsmanship of these exceptional knife-grinders was famous in the Rendeva Valley and beyond. At the gates of the town stands a bronze statue that reminds us of this long lost traditional profession. At the entrance to the town you will find the beautiful **Genova Valley** with its spectacular waterfalls. Genova Valley is the starting point for challenging excursions across the ancient glaciers of Adamello, and was the scene of the terrible battles of the First World War, remnants of which can still be seen today.

VIA DELLE BOCCHETTE

This is a fantastic and extremely pleasurable excursion across the small Passes or **"Bocche"** (Mouths) of Brenta. It's long exposed berms, rope ladders and metal ropes attract thousands of mountain enthusiasts every season. A long and very difficult route, the Bocchette, must be attempted with the right training and preparation, and a good dose of humility; a quality that is highly appreciated in the mountains.

At Madonna di Campiglio or Pinzolo, just like at Andalo and Molveno, you can find all the information on weather conditions and the practicability of the climb. Whatever your level we would advise you to explore these routes in the

company of the Alpine Guides. As well as suitable high altitude clothing you will need the following equipment: safety harnesses, ropes with snap-hooks for **"via ferrata"**, helmet, crampons and ice pick (in the event that you come across snow).

REFUGES OF *B*RENTA

There are numerous characteristic refuges dotted along the Brenta Range. In the Andalo and Molveno region the principal refuges are: **Croz dell'Altissimo,** situated beneath the homonymous 1431 m peak, **Selvata Refuge** at 1630 m and the **Pedrotti Refuge** at 2491 in the direction of the Bocca di Brenta. Above the town of Cles, situated in Non Valley, you will find the **Peller Refuge.** From San Lorenzo in Banale, begins the beautiful Ambiez valley, where at an altitude of 2410 m, you will find the characteristic **Agostini and Pedrotti Refuges,** ideal stop-off

Agostini Refuge

Brentei Refuge with the Crozzon di Brenta

points for those planning on taking a trip to Cima Tosa. From Val d'Algone, leave your car at the malga (shepherds hut) of Vallon, and take the walkway that passes alongside the Sacco Valley that leads to the 2488 m **Garbari Refuge** at **XII Apostoli** (the 12 Apostles), where you will find a small and characteristic church that has been carved out of the rock. Every year in June, hundreds of people participate in the memorial mass with the **SOSAT**

Crozzon di Brenta

Pedrotti Refuge

choir, in memory of those who died at war. From XII Apostoli Refuge you can take a trip along the enchanting "via ferrata" of **"Castiglioni"**, that leads to the **Agostini Refuge.**
From **Vallesinella Refuge,** just a few kilometres from Campiglio, there are numerous walkways that lead to some of the most famous refuges in the Brenta Range. After roughly half an hour's walk you will find **Casinei Refuge** at 1825 m where you can take the footpaths that lead to the **Alberto e Maria ai Brentei, Alimonta, Tucket and Grostè Refuges.** The latter can also be reached using the chairlift. **Brentei** is a family run refuge owned by the famous alpinist Bruno

Tuckett Refuge

The Twelve Apostles Refuge

Detassis, and is situated beneath Cima Tosa at 2182 m. Here you will discover an incredible panorama of the enormous rock masses of Crozzon di Brenta with its vertical walls and the famous Canalone Neri ravine, a long colatoio that is perennially covered with ice, and one of the most difficult **"via nord"** (northern road) in the Brenta Chain. The recently restructured Alimonta Refuge can be found at an altitude of 2580 m and is the highest refuge in the region. It is an excellent point of departure for those wishing to attempt the "Via delle Bocchette Ferrata", which lies halfway between Bocchette Centrali and Bocchette Alte. In fact, the refuge can be seen from the road that leads from Pinzolo to Campiglio under the shadow of the half moon-shaped Cima Sella and Castelletto. The scene resembles a painting from a book of fairytales. Situated at 2272 m beneath the rocky masses of Cima Brenta, the Tucket Refuge is without doubt, one of the most beautiful in the entire region.

THE TRADITIONAL CUISINE OF THE BRENTA DOLOMITES

Simple and genuine products, fragrances and flavours of ancient recipes, that the influence of neighbouring Austria, with its gastronomic traditions, contributes to enrich even more.

This region has been able to make the most of its mountain cuisine, exalting it with the high quality of its wines. Dumplings of all kinds and colours take pride of place amongst the

traditional dishes and are made from bread, potatoes, flour or buckwheat. These specialities are dominated by "Tortel di Patate", followed by "Strangolapreti" and "Spatzle".

The traditional cuisine, jealously handed down over the centuries, is also largely based on sausages and salamis, game and sweets.

However, there is a considerable Germanic influence and so it is impossible to find a restaurant that does not offer dishes such as "Sauerkraut with Frankfurters", "Knodel", a sort of dumpling with meat and flour and Speck, salted smoked raw ham.

Mushrooms are extremely tasty in this area (over 250 different types grow here) and the honey produced by bees inebriated by the perfumes and colours of the meadows at high altitudes is very aromatic.

TORTEL DI PATATE

Peel the potatoes, grate them, add the flour, salt and mix well. In the meantime, heat the oil in an iron or non-stick frying pan to frying temperature. Take a spoonful of the mixture and spread it with the back of the spoon until it is about one centimetre thick. When the edges turn brown, turn the "tortei" over. When they are cooked, place them on kitchen paper, turn-

Ingredients for 4 people:

- *10 medium-sized potatoes*
- *2 tablespoons flour per potato*
- *1 pinch of salt per potato*

ing them over to eliminate excess grease from both sides. Keep them warm in the oven. They can be served with cured meats (speck, aged lucanica sausage, Venetian sopressa) and flavoursome cheeses (Grana, Vezzena, Puzzone...) beans and cabbage and a good red wine.

"STRANGOLAPRETI" GNOCCHI WITH SPINACH

Cut the bread into pieces, put it in a bowl, pour on the milk to cover and leave to soften. Wash and trim the spinach and cook it without adding water but with a pinch of salt. Drain it very well, chop and transfer to a bowl. Add the bread, after squeezing it well and passing it through the vegetable mill, the flour and the eggs, whisked with a pinch of salt and pepper as desired, and mix thoroughly. Add table-spoons of the mixture to a pan containing boiling salted water and cook the gnocchi until they come to the surface. Dress the gnocchi with the butter, in which you have browned the chopped onion and sage, and Parmesan cheese as desired and serve. The traditional "strangolapreti", typical of Emilia Romagna, do not have

spinach in the mixture and are dressed in other ways, for example with a sausage sauce or a sauce made with porcini mushrooms.

Ingredients for 4 people:

- *1000 g spinach*
- *200 g stale bread*
- *2 eggs 4 tablespoons of flour*
- *1 onion*
- *60 g butter*
- *some sage leaves*
- *grated Parmesan cheese*
- *milk*
- *salt, pepper*

LARDO VENATO RENDENA ON BARBECUED POTATOES AND PINK PEPPERCORNS

Boil the potatoes with the peel and cut into slices of about one centimetre. Brown them on the barbecue, thinly slice the lardo venato and lay in a petal pattern on the potatoes. Dust with pink peppercorns and serve.

Ingredients:

- *potatoes*
- *lardo venato Rendena*
- *pink peppercorns*

From: Ristorante La Botte - Pinzolo

APPLE STRUDEL

Peel the apples and eliminate the cores and seeds, cut them into slices and mix them with the sugar, breadcrumbs, sultanas, pine nuts, rum, vanilla sugar, cinnamon and lemon rind.

Heat the oven. Roll out the dough on to a floured board or worktop (40x26 cm) and then lay it in a greased baking tray or lined with oven paper.

Put the apple filling over the dough and fold over the strudel. Brush the surface of the strudel with beaten egg, decorate it with the remaining dough and bake in the oven.

Dust the strudel with icing sugar.

Ingredients for 1 strudel

- *500 g shortcrust pastry*
- *600 g apples*
- *50 g sugar*
- *50 g breadcrumbs toasted in butter*
- *40 g sultanas*
- *20 g pine nuts*
- *2 cl rum*
- *1 sachet of vanilla sugar*
- *1/2 teaspoon ground cinnamon*
- *1 pinch grated lemon rind*

Editorial conception:
Casa Editrice RotalSele srl
Via Cascina Belcasule, 8
20141 Milano - Italia
e-mail: rotalsele@rotalsele.com

Distributed by:
Orempuller
Fotoedizioni S.r.l.
Via Vittorio Veneto, 4 - 38100 Trento
Tel. 0461 - 93.01.27 - Fax 0461 - 93.00.28

Publishing Editor:
Ermanno Stucchi

Text:
Mauro Orempuller

**Graphic design
and makeup:**
Alberto Grazioli

Photographs:
Mauro Orempuller
Massimo Ruzzenenti

Cartography:
Edizioni Lagiralpina
Via A. Zardini, 12
33034 Fagagna (UD)

© Copyright 2009
Printed in UE
by RotalSele srl - Milan
April 2012